i have, so i give

Julia Lloyd

i have, so i give © 2022

Julia Lloyd

Presentation by *BookLeaf Publishing*

Web: www.bookleafpub.com

E-mail: info@bookleafpub.com

ISBN: 978-93-5744-887-1

First edition 2022

DEDICATION

i dedicate this book to my mother, my grandmother and to my close friend Chloe Palaia. thank-you, Mom and Mimi for loving me unconditionally and raising me to be unapologetically myself and thank-you Chloe, for helping me realize how i've impacted your life and the lives around me

ACKNOWLEDGEMENT

i want to acknowledge Justine Wallace, for her last minute advice, editing and help! as well as, the many loves and losses that inspired these poems-hopefully you know who you are

PREFACE

i wrote these poems for myself. and i wrote these poems for you. i am so grateful to all the people that have helped me, because being taught to accept love and support and comfort, taught me the importance of giving love and support and comfort

i know it's easy to be hard on yourself and we are usually more forgiving to everyone else,

so i want to point out that generosity should be deep-seeded. pulled from your heart and soul

it may seem easily renewable but remember, that whatever you give out must come from within. in order to give, you must have. you must give yourself all the things you need and want in order to give them to someone else

so please, take care yourself

giving comes naturally to me

my mother gave my brother
to my grandmother when he was born,
"i can't do this, please help me"
he was three months too early
she was twenty years too young
by the time i came around
my mother had figured it out
and she gave me everything
and then sum,
and i do mean sum
because it is the sum total of who i am today
because it is what allows
me to give
unconditionally,
to you

sharing is caring

you see,
i was raised with praise
and love
and to love myself
to accept mistakes
and eat cupcakes
you see,
i want to turn that onto you

you, me and photosynthesis

i want to tell you how i healed myself with the
sun
how i sat, digesting its rays and i prayed to a god
i didn't believe in
searching for something i didn't know i needed
i want to tell you—
no, show you—
how i healed in the sun
how i've come to believe in myself
taking life's bullshit
and fertilizing my soul
no longer running,
roots planted
i am digging deep
healing hurts
the sun burns
tomorrow i am darker, older, wiser
i want to show you
that you too,
can heal in the sun
water your own seeds
feed your own soul
you don't have to believe me
but please,
keep reading

seeing is believing

listen to me
don't doubt
don't overshadow my affirmations with your
overthinking
believe me when i say,
you are everything
and then sum

search party of one

i want to help
you find the pleasure
in finding yourself

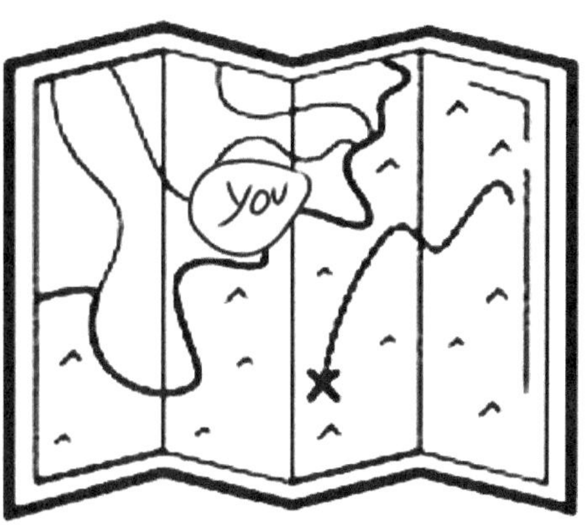

communicate gently

we wouldn't be friends
if you spoke to me
the way you speak
to yourself

one band-aid, please?

i don't think anything hurts
as much as the silence
of you pretending to be okay

the scar tissue
is deep and thick
stiff,
like my emotions

all good things must come to an end

in finding myself,
selfishness was salvation
at least for a little while
it fueled me into embracing my darkness
fooled me into thinking that
darkness wasn't dangerous
lured me
toward a false sense of security
i dove head first into desire
demanding and relentless
it was fun at least for a little while

metaphors and marathons

a gentle reminder to pace yourself
if you want to run, you must walk
if you want to jump, you must stand
i wanted to write, so i wrote
i needed to heal
so i searched
and learned to love the marathon of life
pace yourself
because sprinting
doesn't last
and the future will pass
before you even know it

rise and shine

waking up in the morning
and my bed smells like you
like us
our love
our lust
when i was a young girl
i would lay awake at night
fantasizing about you
except to me you were just a dream
elusive as could be
disappearing at the seams
before the sun could reach me
so now, when i wake up
i am anxious to see
you are still here with me
the sun is bright as we kiss
and i've never been more grateful for
waking up in the morning

you inspire

i hope you know
in this body of yours
you have so much more
to aspire to
than thinness,
soft lips and wide hips
intelligent and radiant
you are the sun,
the moon
the stars
gravitating,
pulling yourself toward greatness
don't waste it
don't change it
don't hate it-
embrace it

leaves and me

i stumbled
fumbling through the pain
standing in the rain
i gained perspective
a new attitude
while drenched in regret and sorrow
i realized that all of what washes over me
also leaves
only soaking up so much
only feeling so many things
so, the rest
i'll let be
and i'll breathe a little deeper
cry a little harder
and feel a lot better

two types of "present"

be present
put your phone down
pay attention
open your eyes
stare wide into the here and now
don't hide
don't sink, scroll, roll
into other people's lives
while yours is passing you by
live and love openly
open your present
unwrap it gingerly, savor the moment
your gift is as good as gone
before you know it

it's okay

it's okay to struggle
to stumble
to fall
to feel
it's okay to heal

take my hand

while my mother gave me everything she had
there were some things she didn't,
some things i had to figure out on my own,
and i believe it was her trust in me
that allowed me to see myself
that allowed me to be myself
i know not everyone is so lucky
i know i am privileged and blessed
and i believe that even if your mother couldn't
or wouldn't do the same for you
you can have everything too
if you want it
let me help
let me share the abundance
of my love and gratitude
with you

selfishness can be salvation

advocate for yourself
your health,
your wealth,
your orgasms,
your wants, desires and needs
don't be shy
speak your mind

seek and you shall find

i know people disappoint, often leaving us
weary and wanting more
weary of our actions that lead us to feeling this
way
wanting to know why others treat us the same
i think it's safe to say,
it's not all sunshine and rainbows
and that's okay
embrace your pain
you won't always get the answers you seek
so, find them in yourself

gazing at the fine print

reading between the lines
has always been a skill of mine
i'm more interested
in what you don't say
than what you do

beautifully ugly

life is beautiful
but it is also ugly
and i am unwilling to deny myself
any of the pleasures or pain that comes along
with it
i am more willing to try things than when i was
younger and
i love that growth about myself
the things i want for myself
are also the things i want
for you

some losses are gains

inspired by pain
fueled by the need to heal
surprised by how much healing i really needed
i am wandering, not lost
refusing to settle
i want nothing but the best
i am unwilling to compromise
unwilling to rest
don't test me
i am not in the mood
and i am angry too
demanding what i deserve is exhausting and it's
costing me everything
and giving me so much more
to give to you